# MANCHESTER CITY

## THE OFFICIAL ANNUAL 2019

A Grange Publication

©2018 Published by Grange Communications Ltd, Edinburgh, under licence from Manchester City Football Club. Printed in the EU.

Edited by David Clayton
Designed by Simon Thorley
Photographs ©ManCity (Thanks to Victoria Haydn)

ISBN: 978-1-912595-13-6

# CONTENTS

# CITY'S SUPER HEROES

City set 12 new records on the way to becoming Premier League Champions...

## POW! MOST POINTS

City became the first team ever to reach 100 points in a Premier League season

## POW! BIGGEST WINNING MARGIN

The Blues finished the season an incredible 19 points ahead of second-placed Manchester United, beating the Reds' 16-point margin from 1999/2000

## POW! MOST GOALS

City scored 106 Premier League goals in total, breaking Chelsea's 103 record set during the 2009/10 campaign

## POW! MOST WINS

City won an incredible 32 matches in the Premier League – two ahead of Chelsea from the 2016/17 campaign

# POW!
## NEW CLUB RECORD

The previous Club record of 31 wins from 2001/02 in a single season was eclipsed last season – and it is even more impressive given that was a 56-game season!

# POW!
## YOUNGEST

Phil Foden become the youngest ever player to receive a Premier League medal when City were crowned champions

# CITY'S SUPER HEROES

## POW!
### MOST AWAY WINS

City's away points totalled 50 and included 16 wins and two draws with just one defeat

## POW!
### SUCCESSIVE WINS

City's 18-match winning streak before the New Year smashed the Premier League record of successive wins

## POW!
### MOST POSSESSION

City's 82.1% possession stat against Everton in March 2017 is the highest ever recorded

# POW!
## EARLIEST TITLE WIN
City's title win with five games to go equals the record set by Manchester United in 2000/01

# POW!
## GOAL DIFFERENCE
City finished with a goal difference of +79, beating Chelsea's previous high set in 2009/2010

# POW!
## MOST OPPONENTS BEATEN
City beat every team in the Premier League at least once during the 2017/18 season, becoming only the third team in history to beat every other side in the league in the season

IHAD
RWAYS

# CHAMPIONS!

## THESE ARE THE MOMENTS
## WE REMEMBER...

More than 100,000 people crammed the Manchester
city centre to welcome the Premier League Champions
– here are some memorable moments from the parade
and the trophy lift as the Blues were officially crowned...

# SPOT THE DIFFERENCE

**Look closely at picture A and picture B – there are six differences in picture B, but can you find them all?**

*Answers on page 60&61*

# GUESS WHO?#1

**Here are four mystery City players – use your powers of observation and detective work to solve their identity – we didn't even need to disguise them...**

01

02

03

04

*Answers on page 60&61*

# HAIR-RAISING

Imagine if you swapped the hair of one City player and put it on another? That's exactly what we've done below – the question is, whose hair are the players below wearing?

Answers on page 60&61

# WORDSEARCH#1

See how many City players you can find in our Wordsearch – remember, the words could be horizontal, vertical or diagonal! There are 10 to find...

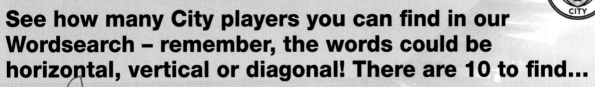

```
B D R E K L A W E L Y K V A
E A L K B V D A N I L O H Y
N N K D T N L K M V V C B S
J I M H L Q L G Y H E W U M
A E B Z P B K R R M N S Z L
M L K E B L N P N B E Q E M
I G M M R W E S P J D R T H
N R T V L N A D L N O F D N
M I C H W K A E N Y F Z Y Q
E M H R U B I R S A L L X Q
N S T L G R V A D X I M Y Z
D H K Z B V N L F O H B H C
Y A R A K E J M Z N P M A N
C W G M V R L G P B M L G F
```

**PHIL FODEN**
**LUKAS NMECHA**
**DANIEL GRIMSHAW**
**DANILO**
**BERNARDO**

**GABRIEL JESUS**
**LEROY SANE**
**BENJAMIN MENDY**
**KYLE WALKER**
**FABIAN DELPH**

Answers on page 60&61

# 2018/19 SUMMER SIGNING: RIYAD MAHREZ

**City completed the signing of Riyad Mahrez from Leicester in July 2018.**

The 27-year-old signed a contract until 2023 and opted to take the number 26 shirt – the same squad number he wore during his four-and-a-half years with Leicester City.

A title winner with the Foxes in 2016, Mahrez was born in France and began his professional career at Le Havre, where he made 67 appearances over a three-year period.

He signed for Leicester in January 2014 and helped them win promotion to the Premier League by the end of his first season. He played 19 times and scored three goals, finishing the season strongly after an initial period of adjustment.

The 2014/15 season saw Leicester finish 14th in the league as they won seven of their final nine league games to save them from what appeared to be certain relegation, but Mahrez was becoming ever more integral in Leicester's style of play and beginning to forge a lethal partnership with Jamie Vardy.

In 2015/16, Leicester won the title comfortably, finishing 10 points above second-placed Arsenal, despite starting the season as 5000-1 outsiders and being many people's tip for relegation.

Mahrez was arguably Leicester's most important player, a fact recognised in the end-of-season awards when he secured a place in the PFA Team of the Year and was named the PFA Players' Player of the Year after scoring 17 league goals in 37 matches.

Mahrez was also named the African Player of the Year and the BBC African Player of the Year in 2016 – a memorable one for the gifted Algerian winger.

In his final two years with the Foxes, he scored 23 goals, but Leicester failed to repeat their 2016 heroics, finishing 12th in 2017 and ninth last season.

In total he played 179 times for Leicester, scoring 48 times – he also created 27 goals for his team-mates during his time at the King Power Stadium.

Mahrez has also won 39 caps for Algeria, scoring eight goals since his debut in 2014.

## MAHREZ FACTFILE:

**Name:** Riyad Karim Mahrez
**Squad number:** 26
**Date of birth:** February 21, 1991
**Birthplace:** Sarcelles, France
**Previous Clubs:** Quimper, Le Havre II, Le Havre, Leicester

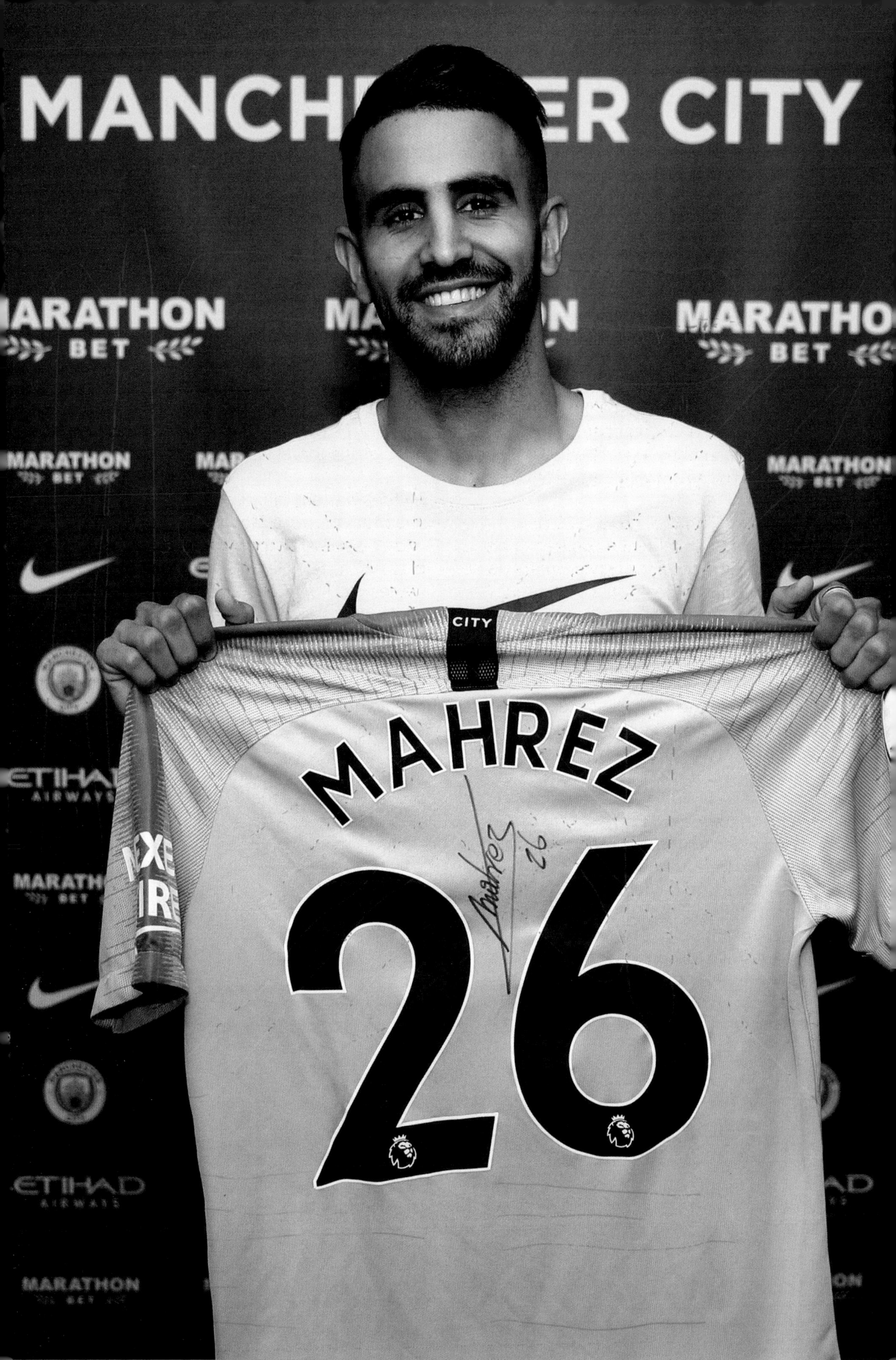
MARATHON
BET
CITY
MAHREZ
26

# CROSSWORD

## Can you solve the puzzle by working out the clues?

Across answers filled in the grid: 4 LIVERPOOL, 6 (down) IKAYGUNDOGAN, 7 BERNARDOSILVA, 14 LEROYSANE

**ACROSS**

2 City's Player of the Season 2017/18
4 Team that ended City's Champions League hopes
5 Stockport-born City midfielder
7 Portuguese play-maker, formerly of Monaco
8 City's main shirt sponsor
10 Nicolas Otamendi's nickname
11 Team City beat in the Carabao Cup final last season
14 City's PFA Young Player of the Year
15 The Blues' Jamaican-born forward
17 Long-serving City first team coach and former player
18 City's French-born Spanish-speaking centreback
19 Famous song City fans sing
20 City midfielder who once played for Shakhtar Donetsk

**DOWN**

1 City first team coach once of Everton and Arsenal
3 City's all-time record goal-scorer
6 City midfielder who used to play for Borussia Dortmund
9 Venue City's EDS and Man City Women play their home games
12 The club Pep Guardiola managed before City
13 Name City were nicknamed after recordbreaking 2017/18 season
16 Number of City players who went to last summer's World Cup

Answers on page 60&61

# SPOT THE BALL#1

We've removed the real ball from the picture below, so you'll have to use detective work to try and figure out exactly which grid it's in – it's tricky and maybe not as obvious as it first looks.

Answers on page 60&61

# HOW TO SCORE THE GOAL OF THE SEASON!

## FERNANDINHO V STOKE CITY
## ETIHAD STADIUM
## 14TH OCTOBER 2017

## 01

It's always best if your team is comfortably in the lead
City were 4-2 ahead at ✓ the time

## 02

It always looks better if you are a long way from goal when you shoot
we estimate Fernandinho was approximately 35 ✓ yards from goal!

## 03

When you receive the ball, you should have at least 15 players (including the goalkeeper) in front of you
in this case, Ferna had 10 ✓ Stoke players ahead of him and five of his team-mates

## 04
**If nobody is closing you down, why not have a pop at goal**
Ferna was so far out the Stoke players didn't feel there was a realistic threat so when he received a pass from Fabian Delph, he had about 10 yards of space in front of him ✓

## 06
**Make your mind up quickly!**
Ferna knew what he was going to do the moment the ball was played to him – he controlled it, nudged it forward and then had a shot ✓

## 05
**If you're going to hit a long-range effort, making it on target, hit it cleanly and with as much power as possible**
Ferna couldn't have hit a sweeter shot ✓

## 07
**If you want to score the best goal of the season, make sure it goes in the top corner of the goal**
the ball flew off Ferna's foot like a missile and arrowed into the top left-hand corner of the goal ✓

## 08
**It helps if you are Brazilian!**
Fernandinho is, we can confirm, a Brazilian! His goal against Stoke was almost exactly the same as a goal scored by Elano, at the same end and with the same spectacular results. And yes, Elano is Brazilian, too... ✓

JILLSCOTT

# WORDSEARCH#2

City have faced a number of top European sides in recent seasons in the Champions League – see if you can find 10 of them in our Wordsearch below...

```
F  K  H  P  T  K  P  A  G  L  Y  M  T  P
Q  A  L  N  K  F  L  R  O  M  K  C  T  A
H  P  M  N  K  L  N  O  F  A  W  D  M  R
T  F  T  O  I  H  P  G  D  N  M  N  T  I
K  M  R  V  R  R  F  W  F  O  S  K  N  S
M  D  E  E  E  S  P  R  G  L  U  T  K  S
K  S  T  V  A  M  A  N  F  E  T  R  L  T
X  V  I  F  L  L  A  T  N  C  N  C  D  G
L  L  W  Q  M  P  M  F  L  R  E  P  Z  E
F  M  T  N  O  Q  X  A  P  A  V  T  K  R
K  J  W  L  D  B  R  Q  D  B  U  X  B  M
G  L  I  D  J  C  N  T  N  R  J  N  G  A
R  B  A  Y  E  R  N  M  U  N  I  C  H  I
D  R  O  O  N  E  Y  E  F  L  W  D  J  N
```

**BARCELONA**

**LIVERPOOL**

**BAYERN MUNICH**

**REAL MADRID**

**PARIS ST GERMAIN**

**NAPOLI**

**FEYENOORD**

**JUVENTUS**

**AS ROMA**

**SEVILLA**

Answers on page 60&61

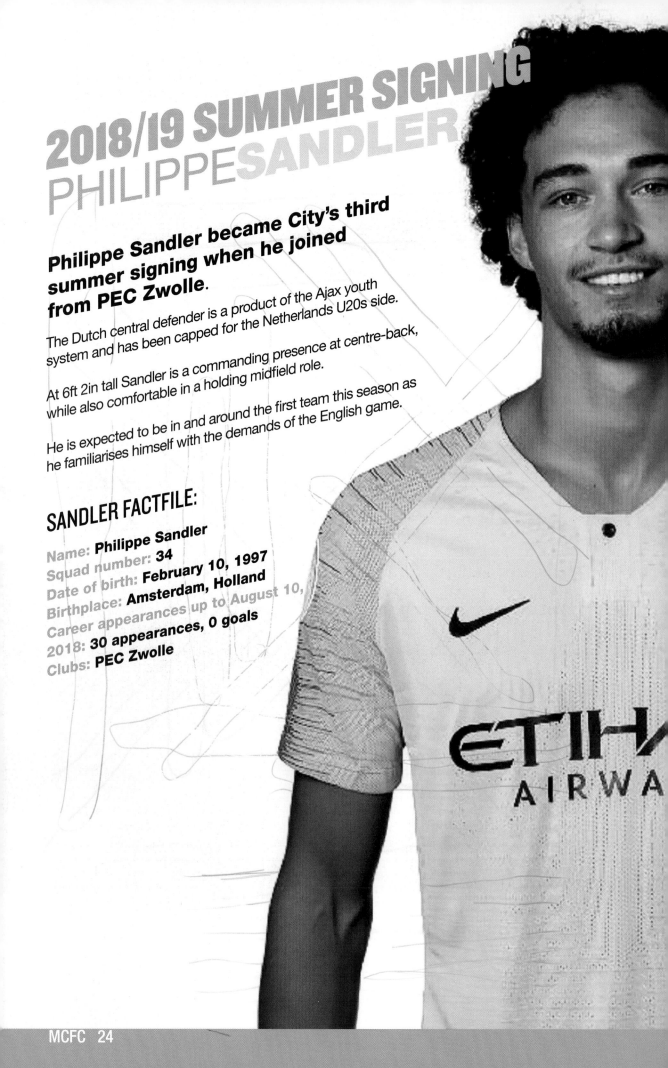

# 2018/19 SUMMER SIGNING
## PHILIPPE SANDLER

**Philippe Sandler became City's third summer signing when he joined from PEC Zwolle.**

The Dutch central defender is a product of the Ajax youth system and has been capped for the Netherlands U20s side.

At 6ft 2in tall Sandler is a commanding presence at centre-back, while also comfortable in a holding midfield role.

He is expected to be in and around the first team this season as he familiarises himself with the demands of the English game.

### SANDLER FACTFILE:

**Name: Philippe Sandler**
Squad number: **34**
Date of birth: **February 10, 1997**
Birthplace: **Amsterdam, Holland**
Career appearances up to August 10, 2018: **30 appearances, 0 goals**
Clubs: **PEC Zwolle**

"Benjamin Mendy holds the Community Shield after City's 2-0 win over Chelsea – the perfect way to start the 2018/19 season!"

# THE BIG CITY QUIZ 2019

**40 questions to test your City knowledge to the max! There's 100 points available – can you become a Centurion – or will you settle for a Champions League spot? All questions relate to the 2017/18 season…**

**01** Who did Sergio Aguero set a new club scoring record against? (3 points)

**02** Who scored City's 100th Premier League goal? (4 points)

**03** True or false? Nicolas Otamendi topped the Premier League passing chart (2 points)

**04** Who had a stunning goal wrongly ruled out away to Cardiff? (3 points)

**05** Which club did Aymeric Laporte sign from? (2 points)

**06** City won two penalty shoot-outs – but who were they against? (3 points)

**07** Benjamin Mendy and Gabriel Jesus were both injured and ruled out for several weeks after playing against which club? (3 points)

**08** Which team inflicted the Blues' only Premier League away defeat? (2 points)

**09** How many Premier League assists did Leroy Sané provide? (4 points)

**10** Who scored City's 100th Champions League goal? (4 points)

**11** Which City player joined Everton on loan in January 2018? (2 points)

**12** How many times was Pep Guardiola voted the Premier League Manager of the Month in succession? (2 points)

**13** Who were the first team to take points off City at the Etihad? (1 point)

**14** Who scored City's first goal of the season? (2 points)

**15** True or false? Aymeric Laporte could have represented Spain instead of France (1 point)

**16** Who made more appearances in all competitions than anybody else? (4 points)

**17** Which club did Ederson sign from? (2 points)

**18** Four City players made 10 or more Premier League assists – can you name them (4 points – 1 point for each)

**19** How many goals in total did City and Liverpool score during the four meetings (Premier League and Champions League)? (2 points)

**20** Who was voted City's Player of the Season? (1 point)

Answers on page 60&61

# THE BIG CITY QUIZ 2019

**21** Who won City's Goal of the Season? (2 points)

**22** Which City player was voted the PFA Young Player of the Year? (1 point)

**23** Which club did Danilo sign from? (1 point)

**24** Which teenage City star scored a spectacular goal in the 4-1 pre-season win over Real Madrid? (4 points)

**25** Which City player became the youngest Premier League champion to receive a medal? (2 points)

**26** Which City defender scored three Champions League goals in the group stages? (2 points)

**27** Name the two teams that stopped City scoring at home? (4 points)

**28** What was the final aggregate score between City and Bristol City in the Carabao Cup semi-final? (3 points)

**29** City beat Wolves on penalties in the Carabao Cup – by what score? (4 points)

**30** Who was the scorer of Wigan's goal in the 1-0 FA Cup defeat? (2 points)

**31** Which team did City beat 3-0 twice in the space of five days? (2 points)

**32** How many games did City win in succession to create a new Premier League record? (4 points)

**33** Who ended the above run? (2 points)

**34** How many City career goals did Sergio Aguero end the 2017/18 season on? (3 points)

**35** True or false: City beat every Premier League team at some stage last season (1 point)

**36** How many Premier League clean sheets did Ederson keep? 10, 13 or 15? (3 points)

**37** Who was sent off on his home debut? (2 points)

**38** Who was sent off during the FA Cup tie with Wigan? (2 points)

**39** Who was sent off after celebrating a late winner at Bournemouth? (2 points)

**40** Who won the FIFA Under-17 World Cup Golden Ball? (3 points)

HOW MANY DID YOU SCORE?

0-25 FREE TRANSFER!
26-50 EXTRA TRAINING BUT DECENT EFFORT
51-75 NEW CONTRACT OFFER!
76-100 PLAYER OF THE YEAR!

Answers on page 60&61

# SPOT THE BALL#2

**Can you spot the ball? We've removed the real ball from the picture below so you'll have to use detective work to try and figure out exactly which grid it's in – it's tricky and maybe not as obvious as it first looks.**

*Answers on page 60&61*

# NAME GAME

There are 10 names below associated with City – they could be players or part of the coaching staff – can you unjumble the letters to find their identity?

HI BIZ DRAMA

R ELK KEY LAW

U DROP AIL PAGE

MET RAIL TAKE

ROSE DEN

ABA FIND HELP

REAL YES NO

OAT CRIME PLAYER

RED SOIL VAN BAR

I SLUG JAR BEES

Answers on page 60&61

GABRIEL JESUS

AYMERIC **LAPORTE**

# 2018/19 SUMMER SIGNING: CLAUDIO GOMES

## Claudio Gomes joined City in July 2018.

The 18-year-old French defensive midfielder was previously with Paris Saint-Germain, making five appearances for the Ligue 1 champions' Under-23 side in the UEFA Youth League.

The highly-rated teenager has also represented France at various youth levels and is the current captain of Les Bleus' Under-18s team. Gomes is quick, strong and an excellent tackler with great vision and energy.

He featured in the summer tour of the USA and made his debut in the closing moments of the Charity Shield win over Chelsea.

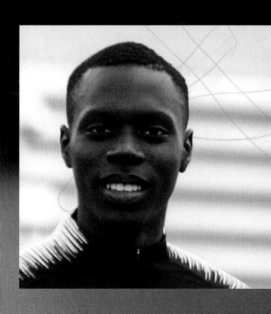

## GOMES FACTFILE:

**Name:** Claudio Gomes
**Squad number:** 81
**Date of birth:** July 23, 2000
**Birthplace:** Argenteuil, France
**Career appearances up to August 10, 2018:**
1 appearance, 0 goals
**Clubs:** PSG
**Honours:** FA Community Shield

# FUNNIES

Everyone knows how hard City work on the training ground, but under Pep Guardiola, there are always plenty of smiles and laughter – as our gallery here shows!

"Just an inch to the right and then launch it!"

City take grass roots football very seriously...

"If I stretch your arms a bit more you could make a great keeper, Bernardo."

Tosin Adarabioyo reckons there's too much rabbiting going on here...

Kevin De Bruyne reacts to John Stones' singing 'Football's coming home.'

"I think there might be too much static in these tracksuit tops..."

# THEY SAY EVERY PICTURE TELLS A STORY

No words are necessary in our comic book-style recap of the 3-0 CARABAO CUP final win over Arsenal last season...

# WORDSEARCH#3

In our third and final Wordsearch, see if you can find 10 things you might eat or drink on a match day...

```
E D G M L W N M L F N N Z S E
T B O Q P L S P S I R C P I N
A Y D D T R T J K L H I P K R
L H T R K L W L K T H I K E L
O A O W T Q W L M C T X G T M
C M H R M X R W D L K R L K F
O B M R V G Z N A R U V M D R
H U W B N K A B Q B D X X T L
C R K M W H N L E K D W G E V
T G F B S E K S R B L W M M W
O E G I K N E N T G C O R X K
H R F C Y E X F Q W N H K N T
Q P I C H O C O L A T E I P L
M H J C L T N N D N N Q M P K
C M Z T H X W E W L L Q X D S
```

**HOT DOG**

**CHICKEN BALTI PIE**

**CHOCOLATE**

**CHIPS**

**HAMBURGER**

**LEMONADE**

**CHEESEBURGER**

**CRISPS**

**HOT CHOCOLATE**

**FISH AND CHIPS**

Answers on page 60&61

PHIL**FODEN**

# ASSISTKINGS

For the first time in the Premier League era, one club dominated the top of the assists charts for league games – City!

The Blues had the top four positions in the 2017/18 Premier League end of season top 10 – a fantastic achievement for our selfless creative geniuses.

So, here's their incredible season stats with the dream quartet creating no less than 53 goals!

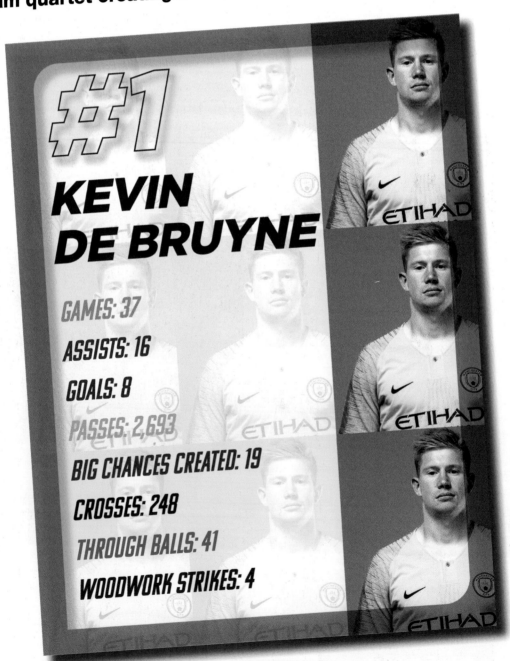

## #1 KEVIN DE BRUYNE

GAMES: 37

ASSISTS: 16

GOALS: 8

PASSES: 2,693

BIG CHANCES CREATED: 19

CROSSES: 248

THROUGH BALLS: 41

WOODWORK STRIKES: 4

## LEROY SANE

**GAMES:** 32 **ASSISTS:** 15 **GOALS:** 10 **PASSES:** 1,091
**BIG CHANCES CREATED:** 13 **CROSSES:** 93
**THROUGH BALLS:** 0 **WOODWORK STRIKES:** 2

# #2

## RAHEEM STERLING

**GAMES:** 33 **ASSISTS:** 11 **GOALS:** 18 **PASSES:** 1,170
**BIG CHANCES CREATED:** 11 **CROSSES:** 39
**WOODWORK STRIKES:** 4

# #3

## DAVID SILVA

**GAMES:** 29 **ASSISTS:** 11 **GOALS:** 9 **PASSES:** 2,429
**BIG CHANCES CREATED:** 14 **CROSSES:** 74
**WOODWORK STRIKES:**

# #4

# MCFC WOMEN: SEASON 2017/18

**It was a case of so near yet so far for Nick Cushing's Manchester City Women during the 2017/18 season....**

There was much to admire from the defending FA Women's Super League champions, but the Blues just fell short in all four competitions despite coming so close.

In the League, City were the top scorers and had the second-best defence, but it was Chelsea who took the title after ending the campaign unbeaten.

## TOP MAN CITY WOMEN SCORERS (FAWSL)

| PLAYERS | GAMES | GOALS |
| --- | --- | --- |
| NIKITA PARRIS | 24 | 14 |
| ISOBEL CHRISTIANSEN | 24 | 12 |
| CLAIRE EMSLIE | 24 | 8 |
| GEORGIA STANWAY | 19 | 8 |
| JILL SCOTT | 22 | 7 |
| NADIA NADIM | 14 | 5 |
| JANE ROSS | 18 | 5 |
| JENNIFER BEATTIE | 25 | 4 |
| STEPHANIE HOUGHTON | 21 | 2 |

City drew both games with Chelsea and ended six points behind the West Londoners.

Yet the Blues had started in superb fashion, winning the first seven matches, scoring 27 goals – but just five more wins in the 11 games that remained allowed those trailing in City's wake to catch up and, in Chelsea's case, eventually take over.

The Continental Tyres Cup offered the chance of some early silverware, but though City reached the final, it was Arsenal who triumphed 1-0.

The FA Women's Cup saw City beaten 2-0 by old rivals Chelsea and so the UEFA Women's Champions League was the last chance of a knock-out trophy.

City cruised through the first three rounds to set up another two-legged semi-final with Lyon – the side that had ended the Blues' hopes at the same stage last season.

The first game ended 0-0 at the Academy Stadium and in the cruellest of circumstances, former City defender Lucy Bronze scored the only goal in the second leg to give Lyon a 1-0 overall win and a win over Wolfsburg in the final gave the French powerhouse yet another Champions League title.

The 2018/19 season will see new signings such as Lauren Hemp and Caroline Weir bolster the squad – and don't be surprised if one or two trophies end up back with the Blues next season!

# SOCIAL MEDIA KINGS

## So, who are City's most active social media stars?

We looked at two social media platforms to find out – Twitter and Instagram – and it was interesting to see a lot of the more senior players have bigger followings on Twitter while the younger players have much bigger Instagram followings.
Our two lists show the numbers involved….

 ## Twitter: Top 20

| | |
|---|---|
| SERGIO AGUERO | 13.2MILLION |
| DAVID SILVA | 3.79MILLION |
| VINCENT KOMPANY | 2.93MILLION |
| CLAUDIO BRAVO | 1.92MILLION |
| FERNANDINHO | 1.54MILLION |
| KYLE WALKER | 1.8MILLION |
| KEVIN DE BRUYNE | 1.44MILLION |
| RAHEEM STERLING | 1.43MILLION |
| LEROY SANE | 1.05MILLION |
| BENJAMIN MENDY | 830,000 |
| ILKAY GUNDOGAN | 806,000 |
| NICOLAS OTAMENDI | 560,000 |
| GABRIEL JESUS | 511,000 |
| BERNARDO SILVA | 310,000 |
| EDERSON | 86,000 |
| DANILO | 65,000 |
| PHIL FODEN | 64,000 |
| BRAHIM DIAZ | 44,000 |
| TOSIN ADARABIOYO | 23,400 |
| DANIEL GRIMSHAW | 2,400 |

 ## Instagram: Top 20

| | |
|---|---|
| SERGIO AGUERO | 9.1MILLION |
| GABRIEL JESUS | 7.6MILLION |
| KEVIN DE BRUYNE | 6MILLION |
| CLAUDIO BRAVO | 5.6MILLION |
| RAHEEM STERLING | 3.7MILLION |
| LEROY SANE | 2.6MILLION |
| ILKAY GUNDOGAN | 2.1MILLION |
| VINCENT KOMPANY | 1.4MILLION |
| NICOLAS OTAMENDI | 1.3MILLION |
| FERNANDINHO | 1.2MILLION |
| BENJAMIN MENDY | 1.2MILLION |
| EDERSON | 1.1MILLION |
| DAVID SILVA | 1MILLION |
| KYLE WALKER | 873,000 |
| BERNARDO SILVA | 776,000 |
| JOHN STONES | 525,000 |
| OLEKSANDR ZINCHENKO | 321,000 |
| FABIAN DELPH | 300,000 |
| PHIL FODEN | 233,000 |
| BRAHIM DIAZ | 218,000 |

JOHN STONES AND FABIAN DELPH ARE NOT CURRENTLY ON TWITTER AS OF JUNE 2018

Based on Twitter and Instagram, Sergio Aguero is our social media king with more than 23million followers across our two chosen platforms with Gabriel Jesus next on 8.1million and Claudio Bravo on 7.52million and Kevin De Bruyne on 7.44million.
Next season we'll add Facebook to the above lists!

# 2017/18 STATS

The Premier League table from last season made happy reading – and here's why – City had the best home and away record from the 38 games played as the Centurions smashed record after record....

## PREMIER LEAGUE TABLE – HOME AND AWAY STATS

### HOME TABLE

| | | Games | W | D | L | GF | GA | GD | Pts |
|---|---|---|---|---|---|---|---|---|---|
| 01 | Man City | 19 | 16 | 2 | 1 | 61 | 14 | +47 | 50 |
| 02 | Arsenal | 19 | 15 | 2 | 2 | 54 | 20 | +34 | 47 |
| 03 | Man United | 19 | 15 | 2 | 2 | 38 | 9 | +29 | 47 |
| 04 | Liverpool | 19 | 12 | 7 | 0 | 45 | 10 | +35 | 43 |
| 05 | Tottenham | 19 | 13 | 4 | 2 | 40 | 16 | +24 | 43 |
| 06 | Chelsea | 19 | 11 | 4 | 4 | 30 | 16 | +14 | 37 |
| 07 | Everton | 19 | 10 | 4 | 5 | 28 | 22 | +6 | 34 |
| 08 | Brighton | 19 | 7 | 8 | 4 | 24 | 25 | -1 | 29 |
| 09 | Newcastle | 19 | 8 | 4 | 7 | 21 | 17 | +4 | 28 |
| 10 | Leicester City | 19 | 7 | 6 | 6 | 25 | 22 | +3 | 27 |
| 11 | West Ham | 19 | 7 | 6 | 6 | 24 | 26 | -2 | 27 |
| 12 | Watford | 19 | 7 | 6 | 6 | 27 | 31 | -4 | 27 |
| 13 | Crystal Palace | 19 | 7 | 5 | 7 | 29 | 27 | +2 | 26 |
| 14 | Burnley | 19 | 7 | 5 | 7 | 16 | 17 | -1 | 26 |
| 15 | Bournemouth | 19 | 7 | 5 | 7 | 26 | 30 | -4 | 26 |
| 16 | Huddersfield | 19 | 6 | 5 | 8 | 16 | 25 | -9 | 23 |
| 17 | Swansea City | 19 | 6 | 3 | 10 | 17 | 24 | -7 | 21 |
| 18 | Stoke City | 19 | 5 | 5 | 9 | 20 | 30 | -10 | 20 |
| 19 | Southampton | 19 | 4 | 7 | 8 | 20 | 26 | -6 | 19 |
| 20 | West Brom | 19 | 3 | 9 | 7 | 21 | 29 | -8 | 18 |

### AWAY TABLE

| | | Games | W | D | L | GF | GA | GD | Pts |
|---|---|---|---|---|---|---|---|---|---|
| 01 | Man City | 19 | 16 | 2 | 1 | 45 | 13 | +32 | 50 |
| 02 | Tottenham | 19 | 10 | 4 | 5 | 34 | 20 | +14 | 34 |
| 03 | Man Utd | 19 | 10 | 4 | 5 | 30 | 19 | +11 | 34 |
| 04 | Chelsea | 19 | 10 | 3 | 6 | 32 | 22 | +10 | 33 |
| 05 | Liverpool | 19 | 9 | 5 | 5 | 39 | 28 | +11 | 32 |
| 06 | Burnley | 19 | 7 | 7 | 5 | 20 | 22 | -2 | 28 |
| 07 | Leicester City | 19 | 5 | 5 | 9 | 31 | 38 | -7 | 20 |
| 08 | Bournemouth | 19 | 4 | 6 | 9 | 19 | 31 | -12 | 18 |
| 09 | Crystal Palace | 19 | 4 | 6 | 9 | 16 | 28 | -12 | 18 |
| 10 | Southampton | 19 | 3 | 8 | 8 | 17 | 30 | -13 | 17 |
| 11 | Arsenal | 19 | 4 | 4 | 11 | 20 | 31 | -11 | 16 |
| 12 | Newcastle | 19 | 4 | 4 | 11 | 18 | 30 | -12 | 16 |
| 13 | West Ham | 19 | 3 | 6 | 10 | 24 | 42 | -18 | 15 |
| 14 | Everton | 19 | 3 | 6 | 10 | 16 | 36 | -20 | 15 |
| 15 | Watford | 19 | 4 | 2 | 13 | 17 | 33 | -16 | 14 |
| 16 | Huddersfield | 19 | 3 | 5 | 11 | 12 | 33 | -21 | 14 |
| 17 | West Brom | 19 | 3 | 4 | 12 | 10 | 27 | -17 | 13 |
| 18 | Stoke City | 19 | 2 | 7 | 10 | 15 | 38 | -23 | 13 |
| 19 | Swansea City | 19 | 2 | 6 | 11 | 11 | 32 | -21 | 12 |
| 20 | Brighton | 19 | 2 | 5 | 12 | 10 | 29 | -19 | 11 |

## EDERSON

**NAME:** EDERSON MORAES
**POSITION:** GOALKEEPER
**SQUAD NUMBER:** 31

**DATE OF BIRTH:** 17/08/1993
**PREVIOUS CLUBS:** RIO AVE, BENFICA

**2017/18 APPS (ALL COMPS):** 45
**2017/18 GOALS (ALL COMPS):** 0
**TOTAL CITY CAREER:**
PLAYED: 45 GOALS: 0

## CLAUDIOBRAVO

**NAME:** CLAUDIO BRAVO
**POSITION:** GOALKEEPER
**SQUAD NUMBER:** 1

**DATE OF BIRTH:** 13/04/1983
**PREVIOUS CLUBS:** COLO COLO, REAL
SOCIEDAD, BARCELONA

**2017/18 APPS (ALL COMPS):** 13
**2017/18 GOALS (ALL COMPS):** 0
**TOTAL CITY CAREER:**
PLAYED: 43 GOALS: 0

# DANIEL GRIMSHAW

**NAME:** DANIEL GRIMSHAW
**POSITION:** GOALKEEPER
**SQUAD NUMBER:** 32

**DATE OF BIRTH:** 16/01/1998
**PREVIOUS CLUBS:** ACADEMY

**2017/18 APPS (ALL COMPS):** 0
**2017/18 GOALS (ALL COMPS):** 0
**TOTAL CITY CAREER:** 0
PLAYED: 0 GOALS: 0

# BENJAMIN MENDY

**NAME:** BENJAMIN MENDY
**POSITION:** LEFT-BACK
**SQUAD NUMBER:** 22

**DATE OF BIRTH:** 17/07/1994
**PREVIOUS CLUBS:** LE HAVRE,
MARSEILLE, MONACO

**2017/18 APPS (ALL COMPS):** 7
**2017/18 GOALS (ALL COMPS):** 0
**TOTAL CITY CAREER:** 0
PLAYED: 7 GOALS: 0

## KYLEWALKER

**NAME:** KYLE WALKER
**POSITION:** RIGHT-BACK
**SQUAD NUMBER:** 2

**DATE OF BIRTH:** 28/05/1990
**PREVIOUS CLUBS:** SHEFFIELD UNITED, NORTHAMPTON (LOAN), SPURS, SHEFFIELD UNITED (LOAN), QPR (LOAN), ASTON VILLA (LOAN)

**2017/18 APPS (ALL COMPS):** 48
**2017/18 GOALS (ALL COMPS):** 0
**TOTAL CITY CAREER:**
PLAYED: 48 GOALS: 0

## DANILO

**NAME:** DANILO
**POSITION:** RIGHT-BACK
**SQUAD NUMBER:** 3

**DATE OF BIRTH:** 15/07/1991
**PREVIOUS CLUBS:** AMERICA MINEIRO, SANTOS, PORTO, REAL MADRID

**2017/18 APPS (ALL COMPS):** 38
**2017/18 GOALS (ALL COMPS):** 3
**TOTAL CITY CAREER:**
PLAYED: 38 GOALS: 3

# VINCENTKOMPANY

**NAME:** VINCENT KOMPANY (CAPTAIN)
**POSITION:** CENTRAL DEFENDER
**SQUAD NUMBER:** 4

**DATE OF BIRTH:** 10/04/1986
**PREVIOUS CLUBS:** ANDERLECHT, SV HAMBURG

**2017/18 APPS (ALL COMPS):** 20
**2017/18 GOALS (ALL COMPS):** 2
**TOTAL CITY CAREER:**
PLAYED: 313 GOALS: 19

# JOHNSTONES

**NAME:** JOHN STONES
**POSITION:** CENTRAL DEFENDER
**SQUAD NUMBER:** 5

**DATE OF BIRTH:** 28/05/1994
**PREVIOUS CLUBS:** BARNSLEY, EVERTON

**2017/18 APPS (ALL COMPS):** 29
**2017/18 GOALS (ALL COMPS):** 3
**TOTAL CITY CAREER:**
PLAYED: 70 GOALS: 5

## NICOLASOTAMENDI

**NAME:** NICOLAS OTAMENDI
**POSITION:** CENTRAL DEFENDER
**SQUAD NUMBER:** 30

**DATE OF BIRTH:** 12/02/1988
**PREVIOUS CLUBS:** VELEZ SARSFIELD, PORTO, VALENCIA, ATLETICO MINEIRO (LOAN)

**2017/18 APPS (ALL COMPS):** 46
**2017/18 GOALS (ALL COMPS):** 5
**TOTAL CITY CAREER:**
PLAYED: 137 GOALS: 7

## AYMERICLAPORTE

**NAME:** AYMERIC LAPORTE
**POSITION:** CENTRAL DEFENDER
**SQUAD NUMBER:** 14

**DATE OF BIRTH:** 27/05/1994
**PREVIOUS CLUBS:** BASCONIA, ATHLETIC BILBAO

**2017/18 APPS (ALL COMPS):** 13
**2017/18 GOALS (ALL COMPS):** 0
**TOTAL CITY CAREER:**
PLAYED: 13 GOALS: 0

# FABIANDELPH

**NAME:** FABIAN DELPH
**POSITION:** MIDFIELDER
**SQUAD NUMBER:** 18

**DATE OF BIRTH:** 21/11/1989
**PREVIOUS CLUBS:** LEEDS UNITED, ASTON VILLA

**2017/18 APPS (ALL COMPS):** 29
**2017/18 GOALS (ALL COMPS):** 1
**TOTAL CITY CAREER:**
PLAYED: 69 GOALS: 5

# FERNANDINHO

**NAME:** FERNANDINHO
**POSITION:** MIDFIELDER
**SQUAD NUMBER:** 25

**DATE OF BIRTH:** 04/05/1985
**PREVIOUS CLUBS:** ATLÉTICO PARANAENSE, SHAKHTAR DONETSK

**2017/18 APPS (ALL COMPS):** 48
**2017/18 GOALS (ALL COMPS):** 5
**TOTAL CITY CAREER:**
PLAYED: 231 GOALS: 75

## ILKAYGUNDOGAN

**NAME:** ILKAY GUNDOGAN
**POSITION:** MIDFIELDER
**SQUAD NUMBER:** 8

**DATE OF BIRTH:** 24/10/1990
**PREVIOUS CLUBS:** VFL BOCHUM, FC NURNBERG, BORUSSIA DORTMUND

**2017/18 APPS (ALL COMPS):** 48
**2017/18 GOALS (ALL COMPS):** 6
**TOTAL CITY CAREER:**
PLAYED: 64 GOALS: 11

## PHILFODEN

**NAME:** PHIL FODEN
**POSITION:** MIDFIELDER
**SQUAD NUMBER:** 47

**DATE OF BIRTH:** 28/05/2000
**PREVIOUS CLUBS:** ACADEMY

**2017/18 APPS (ALL COMPS):** 10
**2017/18 GOALS (ALL COMPS):** 0
**TOTAL CITY CAREER:**
PLAYED: 10 GOALS: 0

# LEROY SANE

**NAME:** LEROY SANE
**POSITION:** WINGER
**SQUAD NUMBER:** 19

**DATE OF BIRTH:** 11/01/1996
**PREVIOUS CLUBS:** SCHALKE 04

**2017/18 APPS (ALL COMPS):** 49
**2017/18 GOALS (ALL COMPS):** 14
**TOTAL CITY CAREER:**
PLAYED: 86 GOALS: 23

# DAVID SILVA

**NAME:** DAVID SILVA
**POSITION:** ATTACKING MIDFIELDER
**SQUAD NUMBER:** 21

**DATE OF BIRTH:** 08/01/1986
**PREVIOUS CLUBS:** VALENCIA, EIBAR
(LOAN), CELTA VIGO (LOAN)

**2017/18 APPS (ALL COMPS):** 40
**2017/18 GOALS (ALL COMPS):** 10
**TOTAL CITY CAREER:**
PLAYED: 346 GOALS: 61

## KEVIN DE BRUYNE

**NAME:** KEVIN DE BRUYNE
**POSITION:** ATTACKING MIDFIELDER
**SQUAD NUMBER:** 17

**DATE OF BIRTH:** 28/06/1991
**PREVIOUS CLUBS:** GENK, CHELSEA, WERDER BREMEN (LOAN), WOLFSBURG

**2017/18 APPS (ALL COMPS):** 51
**2017/18 GOALS (ALL COMPS):** 12
**TOTAL CITY CAREER:**
PLAYED: 141 GOALS: 35

## BERNARDO SILVA

**NAME:** BERNARDO SILVA
**POSITION:** ATTACKING MIDFIELDER
**SQUAD NUMBER:** 20

**DATE OF BIRTH:** 10/08/1994
**PREVIOUS CLUBS:** BENFICA, MONACO

**2017/18 APPS (ALL COMPS):** 53
**2017/18 GOALS (ALL COMPS):** 9
**TOTAL CITY CAREER:**
PLAYED: 53 GOALS: 9

# RAHEEM STERLING

**NAME:** RAHEEM STERLING
**POSITION:** WINGER
**SQUAD NUMBER:** 7

**DATE OF BIRTH:** 08/12/1994
**PREVIOUS CLUBS:** QPR, LIVERPOOL

**2017/18 APPS (ALL COMPS):** 46
**2017/18 GOALS (ALL COMPS):** 23
**TOTAL CITY CAREER:**
PLAYED: 140 GOALS: 44

# RIYAD MAHREZ

**NAME:** RIYAD MAHREZ
**POSITION:** WINGER
**SQUAD NUMBER:** 26

**DATE OF BIRTH:** 21/02/1991
**PREVIOUS CLUBS:** QUIMPER,
LE HAVRE II, LE HAVRE, LEICESTER

**2017/18 APPS (ALL COMPS):** 41*
**2017/18 GOALS (ALL COMPS):** 13
**TOTAL CITY CAREER:**
PLAYED: 0 GOALS: 0
*FOR LEICESTER CITY

## GABRIELJESUS

**NAME:** GABRIEL JESUS
**POSITION:** STRIKER
**SQUAD NUMBER:** 33

**DATE OF BIRTH:** 03/04/1997
**PREVIOUS CLUBS:** PALMEIRAS

**2017/18 APPS (ALL COMPS):** 42
**2017/18 GOALS (ALL COMPS):** 17
**TOTAL CITY CAREER:**
PLAYED: 53 GOALS: 24

## SERGIOAGUERO

**NAME:** SERGIO AGUERO
**POSITION:** STRIKER
**SQUAD NUMBER:** 10

**DATE OF BIRTH:** 02/06/1988
**PREVIOUS CLUBS:** INDEPENDIENTE,
ATLÉTICO MADRID

**2017/18 APPS (ALL COMPS):** 39
**2017/18 GOALS (ALL COMPS):** 30
**TOTAL CITY CAREER:**
PLAYED: 292 GOALS: 199

# GUESS WHO?#2

We have blurred the faces of three City players, can you figure out who they are?

Answers on page 60&61

# QUIZ & PUZZLE ANSWERS

## SPOT THE DIFFERENCE
(From page 12)

1, Kompany and Delph names mixed up.
2, Mendy grabs hand.
3, No badge on KDB'S pants.
4, No tattoo on Edersons left leg.
5, No Gundogan.
6, No Sane and Delph.

## GUESS WHO?#1
(From page 13)

01 BERNARDO SILVA
02 BENJAMIN MENDY
03 KYLE WALKER
04 OLEKSANDR ZINCHENKO

## HAIR-RAISING
(From page 14)

01 DE BRUYNE'S HEAD / GUNDOGAN'S HAIR
02 EDERSON'S HEAD / BERNARDO'S HAIR
03 WALKER'S HEAD / SILVA'S HEAD
04 SANE'S HEAD / KOMPANY'S HAIR

## WORDSEARCH#1
(From page 15)

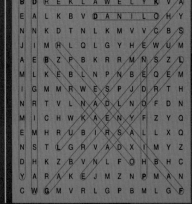

## CROSSWORD (From page 18)

Solution:
KEVINDEBRUYNE
LIVERPOOL PHILFODEN
BERNARDOSILVA ETIHAD
THEGENERAL
ARSENAL GUNDOGAN
LEROYSANE
RAHEEMSTERLING
BRIANKIDD SIX
AYMERICLAPORTE
BLUEMOON FERNANDINHO

## SPOT THE BALL#1
(From page 19)

1  2  3  4

3A X

A
B
C
D

## NAME GAME SOLUTION
(From page 31)

**BRAHIM DIAZ**

**KYLE WALKER**

**PEP GUARDIOLA**

**MIKEL ARTETA**

**EDERSON**

**FABIAN DELPH**

**LEROY SANE**

**AYMERIC LAPORTE**

**BERNARDO SILVA**

**GABRIEL JESUS**

## WORDSEARCH#2
(From page 23)

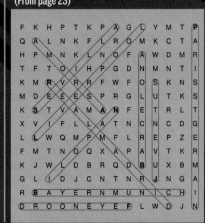

# THE BIG CITY QUIZ 2019

(From page 26-29)

01, NAPOLI
02, PABLO ZABALETA (OWN GOAL V WEST HAM)
03, FALSE – HE FINISHED SECOND TO GRANIT XHAKA OF ARSENAL
04, BERNARDO SILVA
05, ATHLETIC BILBAO
06, WOLVES AND LEICESTER
07, CRYSTAL PALACE
08, LIVERPOOL
09, 15
10, GABRIEL JESUS
11, ELIAQUIM MANGALA
12, 4
13, EVERTON
14, SERGIO AGUERO
15, TRUE
16, BERNARDO SILVA – 53
17, BENFICA
18, KEVIN DE BRUYNE, LEROY SANE, RAHEEM STERLING, DAVID SILVA
19, CITY 9 LIVERPOOL 9 – 18 IN TOTAL
20, KEVIN DE BRUYNE

21, FERNANDINHO
22, LEROY SANE
23, REAL MADRID
24, BRAHIM DIAZ
25, PHIL FODEN
26, JOHN STONES
27, WOLVES AND HUDDERSFIELD
28, 5-3 TO CITY
29, 4-1
30, WILL GRIGG
31, ARSENAL
32, 18
33, CRYSTAL PALACE
34, 199
35, TRUE
36, 15
37, KYLE WALKER
38, FABIAN DELPH
39, RAHEEM STERLING
40, PHIL FODEN

## SPOT THE BALL#2
(From page 30)

## GUESS WHO#2
(From page 59)

BERNARDO SILVA

OLEKSANDR ZINCHENKO

AYMERIC LAPORTE

## WORDSEARCH#3
(From page 40)

# WHERE'S MOONIE & MENDY?
## Can you spot them both?